THE MARRIAGE COVENANT

by

DEREK PRINCE

Copyright © 1978 Derek Prince
ISBN 0-934920-16-8

Background of the Author

Derek Prince was born in India, of British parents. He was educated as a scholar of Greek and Latin at two of Britain's most famous educational institutions—Eton College and Cambridge University. From 1940 to 1949, he held a Fellowship (equivalent to a resident professorship) in Ancient and Modern Philosophy at King's College Cambridge. He also studied Hebrew and Aramaic, both at Cambridge University and at the Hebrew University in Jerusalem. In addition, he speaks a number of other modern languages.

In the early years of World War II, while serving as a hospital attendant with the British Army, Derek Prince experienced a life-changing encounter with Jesus Christ, concerning which he writes:

> Out of this encounter, I formed two conclusions which I have never since had reason to change: first, that Jesus Christ is alive; second, that the Bible is a true, relevant, up-to-date book. These two conclusions radically and permanently altered the whole course of my life.

At the end of World War II, he remained where the British Army had placed him—in Jerusalem. Through his marriage to his first wife, Lydia, he became father to the eight adopted girls in Lydia's children's home there. Together the family saw the rebirth of the State of Israel in 1948. While serving as educator in Kenya, Derek and Lydia Prince adopted their ninth child, an African baby girl. Lydia died in 1975, and Derek Prince married his second wife, Ruth, in 1978. Ruth's three children bring Derek Prince's family to a total of twelve, with many grandchildren and great-grandchildren.

Derek Prince's non-denominational, non-sectarian approach has opened doors for his teaching to people from many different racial and religious backgrounds, and he is internationally recognized as one of the leading Bible expositors of our time. His daily radio broadcast, TODAY WITH DEREK PRINCE, reaches more than half the globe, including translations into Arabic, five Chinese languages (Mandarin, Amoy, Cantonese, Shanghaiese, Swatow), Mongolian, Spanish, Russian and Tongan. He has published more than 30 books, which have been translated into over 50 foreign languages.

Through the GLOBAL OUTREACH Leaders Program of Derek Prince Ministries, his books and audio cassettes are sent free of charge to hundreds of national Christian leaders in the Third World, Eastern Europe and the Commonwealth of Independent States. Now past the age of 75, he still travels the world—imparting God's revealed truth, praying for the sick and afflicted, and sharing his prophetic insight into world events in the light of Scripture.

The international base of Derek Prince Ministries is located in Fort Lauderdale, Florida, with branch offices in Australia, Canada, Germany, Holland, New Zealand, South Africa, and the United Kingdom.

THE MARRIAGE COVENANT

CONTENTS

FOREWORD BY RUTH

Soon after I came to know the Lord Jesus as my Savior and Messiah in 1970, I came into contact with real Christians whose marriages were a constant testimony to His Lordship in their lives. At about the same time, I became acquainted with the teaching and ministry of Derek Prince, Charles Simpson, and others. As a single woman, my prayer to God was, "Set me under authority, in the place You have for me, that I may serve You in the best way, and help to prepare for the coming of Your Kingdom."

My prayers were answered several years later, in a way that I had not anticipated, when God chose me to be Derek's wife, his new helpmeet. Derek's first wife, Lydia, was an extraordinary woman who laid down her life, and her own successful ministry in Jerusalem, for her husband. When Derek married her in 1946 she was a respected spiritual leader there, with an established work of her own.* However, she accepted willingly the behind-the-scenes role of inter-cessor, homemaker, supporter - that of a true wife.

When I first came into close personal

---

*Lydia's own dramatic story is told by Derek in their book, *Appointment in Jerusalem,* published just before her death in 1975.

contact with Derek I was impressed by the way he lives out his teaching in his personal conduct; he "practices what he preaches." I have come to see that much of his present ability to minister to the needs of God's people has its roots in the relationship he and Lydia had with one another for almost thirty years, and in their relationship - as a unit - with the Lord.

Most of the material contained in *The Marriage Covenant* was developed, and taught, before I came into Derek's life. Yet in the same period of time, while I was living in Jerusalem, completely out of touch with his ministry and teaching, the Holy Spirit was speaking to me along the same lines, about the real meaning of "covenant." My study led me to Genesis chapter 15. I identified with the experience of Abraham as he entered into a deep, personal, life-changing relationship with God — a relationship so profound that we still know our God as "the God of Abraham." A life of total commitment.

During the same period, I was also reflecting on the role of women in the Body of our Lord. I saw that God had created Eve for the sole purpose of meeting Adam's need, that man was not complete without his God-given mate. It seems to me that in contemporary western society, and in much of the church, too many women are endeavoring (often loudly) to do something they were never created to do, to succeed in life as independent, solitary entities. For a number of years I myself sought fulfillment in that way, as a career woman. But when I entered into a relationship with Jesus, my life was re-directed. I began to see that it is women who are the losers — along with the men who are not able to achieve the wholeness God intended for them in union with their mates.

I realize that it is not possible for every man and every woman to find that ideal mate, and that certainly it is better to be alone with the Lord than to be unequally yoked with an unbeliever. For many, there is no other choice than to remain single. The quality of the single life, with which I am well acquainted, can be determined by the quality of the relationship with God, and the relationship with other Christians. Commitment seems to be the key, commitment to God, to His will for your life, and commitment to that part of the Body with which you are connected.

It seems appropriate that this book is being published just as Derek and I are joining our lives in the covenant of marriage. At the same time, I am joining myself to the part of the Body with which he is associated in the United States, and he with the part of the Body to which I belong in Jerusalem. We believe we are conforming to God's preordained plan as we each lay down our life for the other, that we may merge into one new entity under the Lordship of Jesus. We know that, as with everything in the spiritual life, this must be walked out on a day-to-day basis. I believe that this book contains not only the pattern, but the practical instruction on how to do so.

I pray that applying the principles of this book will lead you, whether you be a man or a woman, into the wholeness that God wills for you, in covenant relationship with Himself, and with His people.

1

MARRIAGE IS A COVENANT

Is there a secret to a successful marriage? Why do some couples succeed, and others fail? Is it all just a matter of chance?

One thing is certain: if there is a secret that ensures a successful marriage, millions of couples in our contemporary culture have never found it. In almost every country in "western" civilization, the proportion of divorces to marriages has soared dramatically in the last few decades. In the United States we have reached a situation where there is approximately one divorce for every two marriages. Fifty years ago a person familiar with American life would never have dreamed that such a situation could arise in so short a period.

However, the ratio of divorces to marriages does not tell the whole story. Many marriages that have not yet ended in the final shipwreck of divorce, nevertheless find themselves in very troubled and unhappy circumstances. In some cases, there is open strife and disharmony, usually involving all

11

those who live under the one roof, both parents and children. In other cases, although things appear fairly calm on the surface, underneath there are the festering sores of bitterness, unforgiveness, and rebellion. Sooner or later these are liable to erupt in the form of some mental or emotional breakdown, the cause of which may never be precisely diagnosed.

Those who are specifically concerned with mental health have suggested that about one out of every four persons in America today either needs, or will need, some form of psychiatric care. Psychiatric wards in many hospitals are overflowing, and professional psychiatrists are in ever-increasing demand. This has a direct bearing on the condition of marriage and the home, because it is generally agreed that the majority of mental and emotional problems can be traced back to tension and disharmony in the home, primarily in marriage relationships. Thus the progressive deterioration of mental and emotional health is one of many symptoms in contemporary society, all of which point to the most urgent social problem of our day — the breakdown of marriage and the home.

The reaction of certain contemporary sociologists to this situation has taken the form of passively accepting the inevitable. Some have even gone so far as to assert that the concept of marriage was a "mistake" in the first place, and that it is no longer relevant in our present "advanced" state of social progress. However, many of the "experts" who make such pronouncements are themselves the product of unhappy homes; not a few have also the record of at least one unsuccessful marriage in their own lives. We may therefore have grounds to inquire whether their statements to the effect that marriage is "irrelevant" or "outmoded" do not merely put them on the level of the fox in Aesop's fable. He had tried desperately to reach a cluster of luscious grapes, but failed. His final comment was, "Anyhow, they're sour!"

In the face of this confused situation and these conflicting opinions, I want to state, clearly and briefly, my own personal conviction. *I believe that there is a secret that can ensure a successful marriage.* Furthermore, I believe that this secret is revealed in the pages of one unique book — the Bible.

Before I proceed to explain what this secret is, it will be appropriate for me to say a little about my own personal background. This could be interpreted as presenting my "credentials."

Personal Background

I was educated at two of Britain's most

13

famous educational institutions — Eton College and Cambridge University. Prior to World War II I pursued a career in philosophy, and in 1940 I was elected to a Fellowship (i.e., a resident professorship) in this field at King's College, Cambridge. However, the impact of World War II interrupted my academic career.

In 1941, while serving as a hospital attendant in the British Army, I had a dramatic, life-changing encounter with God — something which was totally out of line with my previous philosophic theories and preconceptions. Out of this encounter, I formed two conclusions which I have never since had reason to change: first, that Jesus Christ is alive; second, that the Bible is a true, relevant, up-to-date book. These two conclusions radically and permanently altered the whole course of my life.

In 1946, in Jerusalem, I married a Danish lady, Lydia Christensen, who was the "mother" of a small home for girls which she had founded there. Through my marriage to Lydia I became, in one day, the adoptive father of eight girls, of whom six were Jewish, one was Arab and one was English. Also at this time, for two years, I studied at the Hebrew University in Jerusalem. Lydia and I and our eight girls continued living in Jerusalem throughout the upheavals that marked the birth of the State of Israel. We thus came face to face, as a family, with the grim realities of siege, famine and war. Later we moved, still as a family, to Britain.

In the years that followed, I served in various capacities in various lands: as a pastor in Britain; as an educator in Kenya; as a Bible teacher and conference speaker in Europe, Canada, the United States, New Zealand, Australia and other countries. Throughout all my travels, Lydia was always by my side. Sometimes, after we had been ministering together in public, people would make the comment, "The two of you work together as if you were one person."

In Kenya, Lydia and I adopted our ninth child — an African baby girl. We successfully completed the raising of all our nine girls. All but our youngest have married and have presented us with many grandchildren.

After thirty years my marriage with Lydia was terminated by her death. Our life together had always been an open book — not only to our children, but also to countless people who, through the years, came to our home for counseling and prayer. Of all those who knew us in this way, I question whether there are any who would not agree that our marriage was happy and successful. Certainly it had its fair share of tensions and problems — more than would normally be experienced by a couple who spend their whole life in one familiar setting. But the success of a marriage does not depend upon the absence of tensions and problems; it depends upon a special quality of relationship that needs to be developed between husband and wife.

In the pages that follow, it is my intention to share with you the secret of how to build a relationship of this kind. I trust that the brief outline of my life to this point will be sufficient to demonstrate that my convictions are not just a set of abstract theories which have never been put to the tests of real life.

Perhaps I should add that at the moment of writing I am about to remarry. Coincidentally, I met my second wife Ruth — like my first — in Jerusalem. I enter this second marriage with a quiet trust that, as Ruth and I meet the conditions which God has revealed in Scripture, He will crown this marriage also with His blessing.

Marriage is a "Mystery"

In Ephesians 5:22—32 Paul explains the Christian view of marriage. He concludes by saying, "This mystery is great . . . " He acknowledges, therefore, that marriage is a "mystery." In Paul's time, the word "mystery" had a more specific meaning than it does today. It had a religious association. It denoted a form of knowledge that conferred valuable benefits, but was restricted to a special group bound together by their religious practices. For a person to have access to this knowledge, he had first to be "initiated" into the group.

Thus Paul's use of the word "mystery" to describe the marriage relationship suggests two things: first, that there is a hidden form of knowledge which can make marriage what it ought to be; second, that a person can only acquire this hidden knowledge by undergoing certain tests and meeting certain conditions. It is the main purpose of this book to "initiate" the reader into these tests and conditions.

In the book of Deuteronomy, when the children of Israel were ready to enter into their promised inheritance in the land of Canaan, Moses reviewed for them the kind of life style God had planned for them in their new environment. He promised them, on God's behalf, that if they would keep God's law, they would be abundantly blessed in every area of their lives. In particular, Moses told them that their homes would be like "heaven on earth" (Deuteronomy 11:21 KJV). He painted a beautiful picture of contentment and unbroken harmony. Such was the level of home life God had planned

17

for His people.

About twelve hundred years later, through the prophet Malachi, God took stock of Israel's conduct since they had entered into their inheritance. In general, they had failed to meet God's conditions, and therefore had not enjoyed the level of life He had planned for them. In His assessment, God pinpointed a number of specific areas of failure. One was in their home life, and specifically in their marriages. Here is what He says concerning this, in Malachi 2:13—14:

(13) "And this is another thing you do: you cover the altar of the LORD with tears, with weeping and with groaning, because He no longer regards the offering or accepts it with favor from your hand.

(14) "Yet you say, 'For what reason?' Because the LORD has been a witness between you and the wife of your youth, against whom you have dealt treacherously, though she is your companion and your wife by covenant."

Obviously Israel's failure in this respect was not due to lack of religion. They were "covering the altar of the LORD with their tears." Yet, for all their prayers, their marriages were a failure. We are quite often confronted with a similar situation today.

18

People may be very busy with religious activities, and yet be unable to make a success of their marriages. Their religion does not enable them to succeed at home. Indeed, excessive preoccupation with religion outside the home, by one or both parties, is sometimes an important factor in the failure of a marriage.

The essence of Israel's failure is contained in the closing phrase of verse 14 — "though she is . . . *your wife by covenant.*" Israel had come to view marriage as a relationship for which they might set their own standards — one which they were free to initiate or terminate on their own terms. God reminds them, however, that He views marriage quite differently. According to His unchanging purpose, marriage is a covenant. *This is the secret which alone ensures the success of the marriage relationship.* Once this secret is forgotten, or ignored, marriage must inevitably lose its sanctity and thereby also its strength and stability. Much of what we see in our contemporary civilization is closely parallel to the condition of Israel in Malachi's day, and the root cause is the same — a wrong view of marriage.

Jesus' Standard of Marriage

After Malachi, the next and fuller revelation of marriage comes to us through Jesus. The essence of His teaching on marriage is contained in a conversation He had with some Pharisees, recorded in Matthew 19:3—9:

(3)   And *some* Pharisees came to Him, testing Him, and saying, "Is it lawful *for a man* to divorce his wife for any cause at all?"

(4)   And He answered and said, "Have you not read, that He who created *them* from the beginning MADE THEM MALE AND FEMALE,

(5)   and said, 'FOR THIS CAUSE A MAN SHALL LEAVE HIS FATHER AND MOTHER, AND SHALL CLEAVE TO HIS WIFE; AND THE TWO SHALL BECOME ONE FLESH'?

(6)   "Consequently they are no more two, but one flesh. What therefore God has joined together, let no man separate."

(7)   They said to Him, "Why then did Moses command to GIVE HER A CERTIFICATE AND DIVORCE HER?"

(8)   He said to them, "Because of your hardness of heart, Moses permitted you to divorce your wives; but from the beginning it has not been this way.

(9)   "And I say to you, whoever divor-

ces his wife, except for immorality, and marries another commits adultery.''

We may sum up the teaching of Jesus n this passage in four successive statements:

(1) The form of marriage that had become accepted in Israel under Judaism was below the level of God's will.

(2) God's real purpose for marriage was expressed when He originally created man and woman.

(3) In the initial union of man and woman they were so perfectly joined together that they lost their separate identities and became "one flesh."

(4) It is the purpose of Jesus to restore marriage in the lives of His disciples to the original standard revealed at creation.

If we consider the account in Genesis chapters 1 and 2 of the creation and union of Adam and Eve, one fact is emphasized throughout. God Himself was directly and personally involved. It was His decision, not Adam's, that Adam should have a mate; it was He who formed Eve from Adam; it was He who presented her to Adam; and it was He who established the terms of the covenant relationship in which He united them.

It is, therefore, correct to say that all through the Old Testament marriage was viewed as a covenant relationship. However, the concept that developed under Judaism was on a lower level than that which had found expression at creation. Under Judaism, the covenant relationship was viewed as being merely horizontal — between a man and a woman. But the covenant relationship established at creation had two dimensions — horizontal and vertical. Horizontally, it related Adam and Eve to each other; but vertically it related the two of them together to God.

A Cord of Three Strands

There is a passage in Ecclesiastes 4:9—12 which expresses in allegorical terms the difference between these two levels of marriage:

(9) Two are better than one because they have a good return for their labor.

(10) For if either of them falls, the one will lift up his companion. But woe to the one who falls when there is not another to lift him up.

(11) Furthermore, if two lie down together they keep warm, but how can one be warm *alone?*

22

(12) And if one can overpower him who is alone, two can resist him. A cord of three *strands* is not quickly torn apart.

The principle from which Solomon starts, "Two are better than one," agrees with the reason that God gave originally for providing a mate for Adam, "It is not good for the man to be alone." Solomon goes on to give three examples that clearly illustrate this principle: when two are together and one falls, the other can help him up; if two lie together, they keep each other warm; if two are attacked, together they can drive off the attacker. But the last example that Solomon gives is different: "a cord of three strands is not quickly torn apart." In this case, the strength is supplied not merely by two together, but by *three together.*

We may use Solomon's pictures to illustrate the difference we have observed between the concept of marriage under Judaism and the concept of marriage that was initiated by God Himself at creation. Solomon's first three examples of "two together" illustrate the concept of marriage on the human plane, a horizontal relationship, merely between a man and a woman. But Solomon's fourth picture — the "cord of three strands" — illustrates marriage as it was conceived at creation, a binding together of three persons — a man, a woman, and God. The relationship between the man and the woman is still on the human plane; but when God is added to the relationship, it introduces a new dimension. He becomes an integral part of the marriage.

One of the most revolutionary features of the teaching of Jesus was His standard of marriage. He refused to settle for anything less than the original purpose of God. For this reason, Solomon's picture of a "cord of three strands" not merely illustrates the pattern of marriage established at creation; it also illustrates just as accurately the pattern of marriage for believers today who are united through their faith in Christ. The three strands are the man, the woman and God. The principle that binds them inseparably together is covenant. What Solomon says of a cord thus formed is still true today; it "is not quickly torn apart."

Some time ago I was speaking in New Zealand on this picture of Christian marriage as a cord of three strands. At the end of my talk, a man came up and introduced himself. "I am a professional ropemaker," he said. "My business is making ropes. I want to tell you that what you have said is absolutely true in the practical realm. The strongest rope is a threefold rope."

Then he went on to give me the following explanation: The largest number of strands that can all touch one another is three. If you take away one and leave only two, obviously you weaken the rope. But if you add an extra strand and make four, you do not add to the strength of the rope because all the strands no longer touch one another. If you have a rope of three strands, one — or even two — of the strands may be under pressure and start to fray. But as long as the third strand holds, the rope will not break.

This ropemaker's explanation made the picture of Christian marriage as a threefold cord so vivid for me that I went on meditating on it for days. In my mind's eye I could see the rope under such tremendous strain that two of its strands began to fray. But the third strand remained strong and held out until the strain was eased and the two frayed strands could be bound up.

"That's exactly how it is," I said to myself, "in a truly Christian marriage! There come times of strain when both husband and wife may begin to weaken and feel unable to hold out. But God Himself is that third strand, and He holds on until the strain is eased and both husband and wife can be healed and restored."

In our comparison of Christian marriage to a cord of three strands, we have said that the principle which intertwines the strands and holds them together is *covenant*. Clearly this makes covenant an essential element of a successful marriage. And yet, although covenant is one of the central themes of biblical revelation, it is very little understood by most Christians today. Therefore, we will now go on, in chapter 2, to examine the nature of covenant as it is revealed in Scripture. Then in chapter 3 we will explain in practical terms just how covenant works to unite a man and a woman in marriage and to hold them together.

In chapters 4 and 5, respectively, we will examine how covenant also serves as the essential binding force in two other vitally important relationships: between God and the individual Christian; and between fellow Christians in their relationship to one another.

Finally, in chapter 6, "The Point Of Decision," we will give practical directions to those who feel their need of bringing their personal relationships into line with the principles explained in this book.

2

THE NATURE OF COVENANT

What is there in a covenant that gives to marriage a strength and stability not otherwise possible? What is the essence of covenant?

The nature of covenant is one of the jealously guarded secrets of Scripture. It is a "pearl" which God will not cast to the careless. It is something holy which God will not unveil to the impure. In Psalm 25:14, David says, "The secret of the LORD is for those who fear Him, and He will make them know His covenant." The secret of covenant must be approached in the reverent fear of God. It is withheld from those who approach with any other attitude.

Furthermore, an understanding of covenant requires careful, thorough study of Scripture. It takes time and concentration. In Proverbs 2:4 Solomon states that those who desire discernment and understanding must "seek her as silver, and search for her as for hidden treasures." This implies strenuous effort. Just as the earth does not yield up her treasures to the superficial observer, so Scripture yields up the true understanding of covenant only to those who are willing to go below the surface, and to devote time and study to their search.

I say this by way of introduction to the study of covenant which we will now undertake in this chapter. At first it may seem somewhat hard and laborious. But if we pursue it with patience and diligence, it will ultimately yield up treasures of infinite worth. These will be the subject of the succeeding chapters.

The Definition of Covenant

There are two basic words in Scripture for "covenant." The Greek word used in the New Testament is *diatheke*. The Hebrew word, used in the Old Testament, is *b'rit* (or *b'rith*). This Hebrew word occurs in the name of the well-known Jewish organization, *B'nai B'rith*, which means literally "Sons of Covenant." Each of these words — *diatheke* in Greek and *b'rit* in Hebrew — is regularly translated by two different English words: "covenant" and "testament." The English word used in each case varies according to the context.

In English we do not normally think of "covenant" and "testament" as being the same. We limit the word "testament" to a legal document which — as Scripture points out — comes into force only after the death of the one who made the testament. On the other hand, we do not usually think of a "covenant" as being necessarily associated with the death of the parties to the covenant. However, in the concepts of Scripture, this distinction between "testament" and "covenant" is not valid. In Scripture, a "covenant" is a "testament," and a "testament" is a "covenant."

We are all aware, of course, that the Bible has come to us in the form of two "testaments" — the Old Testament and the New Testament. However, our understanding is increased if we substitute the word "covenant" for "testament" in each case, and speak of the "Old Covenant" and the "New Covenant." It is surely a fact of tremendous significance that God's entire written revelation to man is contained in the form of *two covenants.* Thus the concept of covenant is central to the whole of divine revelation. If we do not understand the nature of covenant, how far can we hope to understand the real meaning of God's message to us?

What, then, is the meaning of the word "covenant?" It is not easy to give a precise and simple definition. It is suggested that the root meaning of the Hebrew word *b'rit* is to *bind*, but that is not certain. It is certain, however, that a covenant is binding. The root meaning of the Greek word *diatheke* is to *set something out in order*. It suggests therefore, the setting forth of specific terms and conditions. It has more of a legal association than its Hebrew counterpart *b'rit*.

In Scripture we find two different types of covenant. One is on the horizontal plane, a covenant between two human beings. This more nearly approaches the concept of a "contract." For instance, Solomon made a covenant with Hiram, the king of Tyre (see 1 Kings 5:12). (The KJV here translates *b'rit* by "league.") By this covenant, Solomon and Hiram committed themselves to mutual friendship and established the conditions upon which Hiram would supply Solomon with material and labor for the building of the temple.

Although this form of covenant was merely on the human level — between two kings — it is interesting to note that later on, when God declared through the prophet Amos that He would bring judgment on the kingdom of Tyre, one reason that He gave was that "they did not remember the covenant of brotherhood" — that is, the covenant made between Solomon and Hiram (see Amos 1:9). So we see that, even on the human level, God considers the breaking of a covenant a very serious matter, and one which will bring judgment on the guilty party.

Covenant:
The Basis of Relationship

However, beyond that, the main use of covenant in Scripture is not as a contract between two human beings on the horizontal plane, but as a relationship sovereignly initiated by God Himself, with man, in which the two parties are not on the same level. Essentially, a covenant expresses a relationship which God Himself sovereignly initiates, out of His own choice and decision. He defines the terms on which He is prepared to enter into that relationship with man. We need to emphasize that the initiative is wholly with God, and the terms are set exclusively by God. Man's part is simply to respond to God's offer of a covenant, and to accept the relationship which that covenant brings with it. Man does not set the terms, nor does he ever initiate the relationship. You have to be something of a Presbyterian, or a Calvinist, to understand this aspect of covenant. Historically, it is the Calvinist stream of Protestantism that has always laid special emphasis on covenant. In so doing, they have preserved a thread of truth which is very important. I would venture to say that we cannot fully understand our relationship with God unless we understand the scriptural concept of covenant.

In the last analysis, every permanent

relationship of God with man is based on a covenant. God never enters into a permanent relationship apart from a covenant. In Psalm 50:1—5, the psalmist gives a prophetic preview of the Lord coming in power and glory at the close of this age to gather His people to Himself. In so doing, He clearly defines those whom God will acknowledge as His people.

(1)　The Mighty One, God, the LORD, has spoken,

And summoned the earth from the rising of the sun to its setting.

[This is a call to the whole earth.]

(2)　Out of Zion, the perfection of beauty,

God has shone forth.

(3)　May our God come and not keep silence;

Fire devours before Him,

And it is very tempestuous around Him.

[This is a clear prophecy of the coming of the LORD in power and glory and judgment.]

(4)　He summons the heavens above,

And the earth, to judge His people;

[This is the judgment of God's people, before the judgment seat of Christ. Not the judgment of the unbeliever, but the judgment of the believer. Not the judgment of condemnation, but the judgment for reward.]

(5)   "Gather My godly ones to Me,
        Those who have made a covenant
        with Me by sacrifice." [This verse
        tells us to whom God's call is ad-
        dressed.]

The Hebrew word here translated "godly one" is *hassid*. It is the word that gives us *hassidic* Judaism — which is the most intense and dedicated form of orthodox Judaism. A *hassid* is a person whose life is totally wrapped up in God. He is a person who exists only for God.

However, the psalmist here defines the "godly ones" — the true *hassidim* — as "those who have made a covenant with Me by sacrifice" — more literally, "those who cut my covenant on the basis of a sacrifice." Hebrew speaks of "cutting" a covenant, rather than merely "making" one. It suggests the action of the knife that puts the sacrifice to death. "My" covenant means specifically the covenant that God Himself initiated, the eternal covenant. There is only one basis on which God makes a covenant — the basis of a sacrifice. Without a sacrifice there can be no covenant.

Years back, about 1944, when I first began to study the Bible in Hebrew, the Holy Spirit prompted me to do something unusual.

33

I armed myself with three colored pencils —
blue, green and red — and I set out to under-
line three different themes with a special color
for each. The themes were: covenant, sacrifice and shedding of blood. Blue was for
covenant, green for sacrifice and red for the
shedding of blood. In that way I stumbled
into a revelation, because I discovered that
wherever I had the blue I had the green; and
wherever I had the green, I had the red. In
other words, wherever there is a covenant
there must be a sacrifice, and wherever there
is a sacrifice, there must be the shedding of
blood.

This agrees with the description of God's
people — His godly ones — in Psalm 50:5:
"those who cut my covenant on the basis of
a sacrifice." Two things are essential for
entering into a permanent relationship with
God: a *covenant* and a *sacrifice*. Without a
covenant there can be no relationship with
God; and without a sacrifice there can be no
covenant.

Historically, the way that men entered
into covenant with God, before the new covenant in Jesus Christ, was very remarkable,
and many people are not familiar with it. It is
referred to in Jeremiah 34:18—20. This is a
period in the history of Israel when they were
backslidden and rebellious in their relationship to God, and they had done something
God forbade them to do — they had made

slaves out of their fellow Israelites. When God reproved them for this through the prophet Jeremiah, they made a show of repentance and entered into a covenant in which they agreed to release their slaves. But then, to add to their sin, they broke their covenant and took the slaves back. The only part of this incident which concerns us just now is the procedure by which they entered into the covenant. This has a significance which goes far beyond this particular moment in the history of Israel. It is described in Jeremiah 34:18—20, where God says:

(18) 'And I will give the men who have transgressed My covenant, who have not fulfilled the words of the covenant which they made before Me, *when* they cut the calf in two and passed between its parts —

(19) the officials of Judah, and the officials of Jerusalem, the court officers, and the priests, and all the people of the land, who passed between the parts of the calf —

(20) and I will give them into the hand of their enemies . . .'

This provides an important addition to our understanding of the process of making a covenant. Not merely did making a covenant require a sacrifice, but the sacrifice had to be dealt with in a special way. The animal that was killed as the sacrifice was cut into two parts, and the two parts were placed opposite one another with a space in between. Then the people who were making the covenant passed between the two parts of the sacrifice. This was the act by which they entered into the covenant.

God's Covenant with Abram

Keeping in mind this procedure for making a covenant, we will turn to Genesis 15:7—18, which describes how the Lord entered into a covenant with Abram (his name had not yet become Abraham):

(7)   And He said to him, "I am the LORD who brought you out of Ur of the Chaldeans, to give you this land to possess it."

(8)   And he said, "O Lord God, how may I know that I shall possess it?"

(9)   So He said to him, "Bring Me a three year old heifer, and a three year old female goat, and a three year old ram, and a turtledove, and a young pigeon."

(10)   Then he brought all these to Him and cut them in two, and laid each half opposite the other; but he did not cut the birds.

(11)   And the birds of prey came down upon the carcasses, and Abram drove them away.

(12) Now when the sun was going down, a deep sleep fell upon Abram; and behold, terror *and* great darkness fell upon him.

(13) And God said to Abram, "Know for certain that your descendants will be strangers in a land that is not theirs, where they will be enslaved and oppressed four hundred years.

(14) "But I will also judge the nation whom they will serve; and afterward they will come out with many possessions.

(15) "And as for you, you shall go to your fathers in peace, you shall be buried at a good old age.

(16) "Then in the fourth generation they shall return here, for the iniquity of of the Amorite is not yet complete."

(17) And it came about when the sun had set, that it was very dark, and behold, *there appeared* a smoking oven and a flaming torch which passed between these pieces.

(18) On that day the Lord made a covenant with Abram, saying,

"To your descendants I have given this land . . ."

The passage opens with the Lord making a promise to Abram that He will give him the land of Canaan for his possession. Abram responds with a question: "How may I know . . . ?" In reply, the Lord proceeds to make a covenant with Abram. In other words, God's final commitment to do anything is in a covenant. When God has entered into a covenant, there is no more that He can do to commit Himself. Covenant represents final, irrevocable commitment. Once God has made the covenant with Abram, He no longer speaks in the future tense. He does not say, "I will give . . . " He says, "I have given . . . " The covenant has settled it — finally and forever.

The procedure by which the Lord entered into the covenant with Abram corresponds exactly to that described in Jeremiah 34:18—20. Abram had to take the sacrificial animals, kill them, and divide them into two pieces. Then it would appear that in due course the Lord and Abram passed between the pieces of the sacrifice. By that strange act, the Lord entered into a covenant commitment with Abram.

Now let us look at some of the details of this transaction. Every one of them is illuminating. Verse 11 — "And the birds of prey came down upon the carcasses, and Abram drove them away." These words bring back very vivid memories to me.

During World War II, while serving with the British forces in Egypt, I lay for one year on end sick and in hospital, with a condition which apparently the doctors were not able to heal. In desperation I turned to the Bible to see what it had to say. Ultimately, after reading the whole Bible through, I came to the conclusion that God had provided healing for me through the death of Jesus Christ on the cross, that it was a part of the covenant God had made with me through Christ. But as I sought to lay hold of this truth, my mind was continually assailed with all sorts of fits of depression and doubt and darkness.

As I lay there, wrestling to appropriate my covenant benefits in Christ, and fighting off these moods of depression and doubt, I happened to read this passage in Genesis chapter 15, and I saw that it was Abram's job to drive the birds of prey away. God ordained the sacrificial objects, but to keep them intact was Abram's job. Likewise, I saw that God had provided the sacrifice in Christ for me, but it was my job to keep those satanic birds from preying on the sacrifice and robbing me of my benefits. So I saw there was a period in which I would have to keep driving the birds away. No matter how many times doubt or unbelief or fear would attack me, it was my privilege and my responsibility to keep those sacrificial objects intact. They were not to be desecrated by the satanic birds of prey that wanted to feed on them and take away from my inheritance.

Then it says in verse 12, "Now when the sun was going down, a deep sleep fell upon Abram; and behold, terror and great darkness fell upon him." This was a very profound spiritual experience in which Abram, as a mature, committed believer, went through "terror and great darkness." Does your theology make room for that? Do you know that some of the greatest saints of God go through periods of spiritual darkness? It is not necessarily a mark of immaturity or weakness to go through darkness. In fact, God cannot trust the immature and weak with that kind of experience. He knows just how much each one of us can endure. Abram did not go through the darkness because he was weak or uncommitted, but he went through it because it was part of his total spiritual experience. His darkness was a preview of what his descendants were to suffer in Egypt. As their father, he had to share a measure of their suffering.

In verses 13 through 16 the Lord explains to Abram what is going to happen to his descendants in Egypt, and how ultimately He will intervene and deliver them, and bring them back to the land of Canaan. Then in verse 17, a new dimension is added to Abram's experience: "And it came about when the sun had set, that it was very dark, and behold, there appeared a smoking oven and a flaming torch which passed between these pieces." To the normal darkness of night is added the blackness of smoke belching from an oven. Frequently in Scripture an oven — or a furnace — typifies intense suffering. In Isaiah 48:10 God says to Israel: "Behold, I have refined you, but not as silver: I have tested you in the furnace of affliction."

This applies at times to all of God's people. If you should ever find yourself in the furnace, remember that is where God refines you and tests you. How you react in the furnace will determine your destiny. You are not necessarily in the furnace because you are weak or backslidden, or because you have failed God. You are in the furnace because the furnace does things for you that nothing else can do. In Malachi 3:3 God warns the sons of Levi — His priests — that He will refine them as gold and silver are refined. Precious metals are never purified without intense heat.

In the midst of this overwhelming darkness to which Abram was subjected — a darkness that was both natural and supernatural — there was "a flaming torch which passed between these pieces." What a depth of meaning there is in that! The flaming torch was a manifestation of the Spirit of God — corresponding to "the seven lamps of fire which are the seven Spirits of God" that John saw before the throne in heaven (Revelation 4:5). It was at this moment —

the moment of deepest darkness — that the Lord, in the appearance of the flaming torch, made His commitment to Abram. He passed between the pieces, and in so doing, He entered into the covenant.

Let me return again for a moment to my experience in the hospital in Egypt. It was at that time of darkness in my own life that the truth of this incident in Genesis chapter 15 became so vivid to me. I learned that there are times of utter darkness when the Holy Spirit will illuminate only one thing: the emblems of the sacrifice. Because that is all we need to see. The sacrifice is the emblem of the covenant, and the covenant is God's final, irrevocable commitment.

You may pass through a time when you can see nothing but the one fact that Jesus died for you. That is all you need to know. Everything is included in that. Romans 8:32 tells us, "He who did not spare His own Son, but delivered Him up for us all, how will He not also with Him freely give us all things?" There are times when that is all you can hold on to. It is the covenant made in the sacrificial death of the Lord Jesus Christ.

So that is how the Lord and Abram entered into covenant. As I understand it, each passed in turn between the pieces of the sacrifices. Isn't it amazing that Almighty God would do that with a man? It staggers my mind that, in a certain sense, God would come all the way down from heaven to pass between those pieces of slain animals, to make His commitment to Abram. I am overwhelmed to realize that God would go to such lengths to make His personal commitment to a man.

Covenant is Valid Only through Death

But why was a sacrifice necessary? Why was that the only way to enter into a covenant? The answer is that the sacrifice symbolized the death of each party to the covenant. As each party walked through between the pieces of the slain animal, he was saying, in effect, "That is my death. That animal died as my representative. He died in my place. As I enter into this covenant, I enter by death. Now that I am in covenant, I have no more right to live." That explains why both Hebrew and Greek make no distinction between "covenant" and "testament."

The necessity of death to make a covenant valid is emphasized in Hebrews 9:16—17:

(16) For where a covenant is, there must of necessity be the death of the one who made it.
(17) For a covenant is valid *only* when men are dead, for it is never in force while the one who made it lives.

These words leave no room for misunderstanding. The one who enters into a covenant enters into it by death. As long as a person remains alive, he is not in covenant. It is impossible to be in covenant and remain alive. The death of the sacrificed animal is physical, but it symbolizes another form of death for the one who offers the sacrifice and passes through the pieces. The one who does this hereby renounces all right, from that moment, to live for himself. As each party passes through the pieces of the sacrifice, he says, in effect, to the other: "If need be, I will die for you. From now on, your interests take precedence over my own. If I have anything you need but cannot supply, then my supply becomes your supply. I no longer live for myself, I live for you."

In God's sight, this act of making a covenant is no empty ritual. It is a solemn and sacred commitment. If we trace through history the course of events that resulted from the Lord's covenant with Abram, we see that each party had to make good the commitment which the covenant represented.

Some years later, when Abram had become Abraham, God said to him: "I want your son Isaac — your only son. The most precious thing you have is no longer yours, because you and I are in covenant. It is mine." To his eternal credit, Abraham did not falter. He was willing to offer up even

Isaac. Only at the last moment did the Lord intervene directly from heaven and stop him from actually slaying his son (see Genesis chapter 22).

However, that is not the end of the story. God had also committed Himself to Abraham. Two thousand years later God, in His turn, fulfilled His part of the covenant. To meet the need of Abraham and his descendants, God offered up His only Son. But this time there was no last minute reprieve. On the cross, Jesus laid down His life as the full price of redemption for Abraham and all his descendants. That act was the outcome of the commitment that God and Abram had made to each other on that fateful night, two thousand years earlier, when they passed between those pieces of the sacrifice. All that followed from then on in the course of history was determined by their covenant.

So solemn, so total, and so irrevocable is the commitment that is made in a covenant.

3

UNION BETWEEN MAN AND WOMAN

In chapter 1 we saw that marriage on the highest plane is "a cord of three strands" — a covenant between a man, a woman, and God. In chapter 2 we saw that a covenant requires a sacrifice; otherwise it is not valid. In this chapter we will apply these principles specifically to a marriage in which believers are united through their faith in Christ.

The sacrifice upon which the covenant of Christian marriage is based is the death of Jesus Christ on our behalf. He is the sacrifice through which, by faith, a man and a woman can pass into the relationship of marriage as God Himself ordained that it should be. Just as the Lord and Abram passed between the pieces of the slain animals, so in marriage a man and woman pass through the death of Jesus Christ on their behalf into a totally new life and a totally new relationship which would have been impossible without the death of Jesus Christ. The covenant of Christian marriage is made at the foot of the cross.

There are three successive phases in the outworking of this relationship. First, a life is laid down. Each lays down his life for the other. The husband looks back at Christ's death on the cross, and says: "That death was my death. When I came through the cross, I died. Now I am no longer living for myself." The wife likewise looks at the cross, and says the same: "That death was my death. When I came through the cross, I died. Now I am no longer living for myself."

Henceforth, each holds nothing back from the other. Everything the husband has is for the wife. Everything the wife has is for the husband. No reservations, nothing held back. It is a merger, not a partnership.

Second, out of that death comes a new life. Each now lives out that new life in and through the other. The husband says to the wife: "My life is in you. I am living out my life through you. You are the expression of what I am." Likewise the wife says to the husband: "My life is in you. I am living out my life through you. You are the expression of what I am."

Third, the covenant is consummated by physical union, and this in turn brings forth fruit which continues the new life that each has been willing to share with the other. In the whole realm of living creatures, God has ordained this basic principle: without union there can be no fruit. Covenant leads to shared life and fruitfulness; life that is not shared remains sterile and fruitless.

This approach to marriage, which sees

it in terms of a covenant, is very different from the attitude with which most people today enter into marriage. Basically, the attitude of our contemporary culture is, "What can I get? What is there in this for me?" I believe that any relationship approached with this attitude is doomed to end in failure. The one who approaches marriage as a covenant does not ask, "What can I get?" Rather he asks, "What can I give?" And he goes on to answer his own question: "I give my life. I lay it down for you, and then I find my new life in you." This applies equally to each party — to the husband and to the wife. To the natural mind this sounds ridiculous. Yet it is, in fact, the secret of real life, real happiness, and real love.

In this new relationship, each party has a special contribution to make. It is noteworthy that in every passage of the New Testament which deals with the mutual obligations of husband and wife, the writer always begins by explaining the special responsibilities of the wife. This is true whether the writer be Peter (a married man) or Paul (an unmarried man). It would seem that, in some sense, the wife is the pivot upon which the whole relationship turns. Unless she plays her part, there is no way that the husband on his own can make the relationship work. We will begin, therefore, by looking at the wife's contribution.

The Wife's Contribution

In Proverbs 31:10—31 Solomon paints one of the most beautiful portraits to be found anywhere in the Bible — that of an "excellent wife." The King James Version translates this "a virtuous woman." Neither translation fully expresses the force of the original. What Solomon really had in mind, I believe, is a woman who knows what it is to be a woman — a woman who knows how to make the fullest and richest expression of her womanhood — a woman who *succeeds* as a woman.

He opens his description with a question — "An excellent wife, who can find?" which would indicate that such a woman is rare. Since I was privileged to share thirty years of my life with a woman who answered to Solomon's description, I can never read this passage without tears of gratitude coming into my eyes.

It is outside the scope of this book to examine every detail of the portrait which Solomon paints. But I want to point out one simple fact which is very significant: the beginning, the middle and the end of the picture all focus on her husband. In other words, the supreme achievement of an excellent wife is her husband. Everything else she achieves apart from that is of secondary value. This is how a woman should measure

49

her achievement as a wife. She is not living out her own life now. Her life is in her husband. She sees her success in him. She rejoices in his achievements more than in her own.

Notice in verse 11 the first statement about this excellent wife: "The heart of her husband trusts in her, and he will have no lack of gain." He does not have to go out in the world and make himself a millionaire to prove himself. His wife's approval is sufficient for him. Many men strive unceasingly for success in business or other fields primarily out of a desire to prove themselves. Usually their root problem is that they never had the assurance of approval in their own homes — first from their parents, and later from their wives. Consequently, they go through life with a driving urge to gain approval and prove themselves. But a man who has the right kind of wife need not depend on anyone else for approval. Hers is enough. Everybody else may misunderstand him, and even betray him, but he knows there is one person on whom he can totally rely. That is his wife. To be a wife of this kind is a very high achievement for a woman.

The husband's trust in this "excellent wife" is based on one simple, but vitally important fact: "She will do him good and not evil all the days of her life." For thirty years I had that total assurance concerning Lydia. She would never do me evil. She would disagree with me, perhaps admonish me. We might argue, or hold different opinions. But I always knew where I stood with her. She was one hundred percent on my side. Without that, I could never have become what I am today.

Let us move on now to verse 23, the central section of this description: "Her husband is known in the gates, when he sits among the elders of the land." Again the focus is on her husband. He is a recognized leader among his people, sitting in the gate — the place of honor and authority. Solomon's language is so expressive. "Her husband is known . . . " In other words, he is known *as her husband.* Without her support he would not have been able to hold the position of honor. This principle holds good in most cases where we see a successful, confident, respected man. A great part of what we are really seeing is his wife's success.

Then, in verses 28 and 29, the description closes with the focus on her family — first her children, but finally her husband once more:

(28)   Her children rise up and bless her;
Her husband *also*, and he praises her *saying:*

(29)   "Many daughters have done nobly,
But you excel them all."

So this description of the "excellent wife" — the truly successful woman — begins with, centers in, and concludes with her husband. He is her supreme achievement, beside which every other achievement is secondary.

What reward does he, on his part, have to offer her? "He praises her." How important that is! Husbands, if you have a wife like this, there is no salary that is adequate for her. You have nothing to pay her with, except praise. And you can afford to be lavish with that form of payment, because the more you pay, the more you receive in return. So take time to praise your wife. Tell her how sweet she is. Tell her how good her food tastes. Tell her how much you enjoy seeing the home so clean. Tell her how pretty she looks. Tell her how much you love her. Take time to do it. It is a good investment. You will get back many times over everything you put in.

For my part, as I have already indicated, I can look back over thirty years of happy and successful marriage with Lydia. If I have one major regret, it is that I did not tell her often enough how much I loved her. I did love her, and she knew it. But I did not tell her as often as I should have. If I could live that part of my life again, I would tell her ten times as often.

Let us return again for a moment to the wife's part. How can a wife achieve this kind of success with her husband? I would say that she has two main responsibilities, closely related to each other. The first is to *uphold* her husband; the second is to *encourage* him.

In 1 Corinthians 11:3 Paul tells us that "the man (husband) is the head of the woman (wife)." In the natural body, final responsibility for decision and direction rests with the head. Yet the head cannot hold itself up. It depends upon the rest of the body to do this. Without the support of the rest of the body — primarily the neck — the head alone cannot fulfill its function.

This applies to the marriage relationship. As head, the husband has final responsibility for decision and direction. But he cannot fulfill this function on his own. He is dependent upon the body to uphold him. In a sense, the wife's responsibility may be likened to that of the neck. She is the one closest to her husband, on whose support he must continually rely. If she fails to uphold him, there is no way that he can function as he should. Just as there is no other part of the body that can take the place of the neck in upholding the head, so there is no other person who can give to the husband the support that he needs from his wife.

The wife's second main responsibility

53

is to encourage her husband. A man should be able to look to his wife for encouragement at all times. Particularly when he least deserves it. If Lydia had only encouraged me when I deserved it, it would not have been what I needed. I needed encouragement most when I deserved it the least. I needed somebody who had faith in me when no one else did. I didn't need a sermon. I didn't need a counselor. I needed someone to trust me.

Encouraging is not an easy thing for a wife to do — especially in times of pressure. It is much easier to reproach or criticize. In fact, encouraging is a ministry that must be cultivated. I believe that many times a wife can transform a bad marriage and an unsuccessful husband into a good marriage and a successful husband, if she will learn how to encourage. But that always means self-denial. We cannot encourage others when we are primarily interested in ourselves. If you and your husband are both feeling miserable, what are you going to do? Tell him how miserable you are? Or encourage him? To encourage him requires self-denial. But that is the essence of the marriage covenant. You are no longer living for yourself.

This brings us back to our starting point — covenant commitment. This alone can provide the grace and the power that each party in a marriage needs to make it successful. Good advice or a set of rules are not sufficient by themselves to do this. There are a number of excellent books available today which offer counsel and instruction from a Christian viewpoint on how to have a successful marriage. But in the last resort, Christian marriage will not work without the supernatural grace of God; and this grace is received only as husband and wife yield themselves to God and to one another in covenant commitment.

The Husband's Contribution

Now we will consider the husband's contribution to the marriage covenant. A good starting place is provided by the words of Paul in 1 Corinthians 11:7: "For a man ought not to have his head covered, since he is the image and glory of God; but the woman is the glory of man."

It is the closing statement that we are concerned with just now — "the woman (wife) is the glory of the man (husband)." This simply takes the same principle that has been applied to the wife, and applies it to the husband as well. We have already seen that the success of the wife is manifested in the husband. Now, Paul tells us, the wife is the evidence of the husband's success. She is his glory — his greatest achievement. Uniquely and supremely, she demonstrates the quality of her husband.

A well-known evangelist was once asked about a fellow believer, "What kind of a Christian is he?" "I can't tell you yet," he replied, "I haven't met his wife." That was a wise answer! Personally, I would never form an estimate of a married man until I had come to know his wife. Because she is his glory. If she is radiant and restful and secure, her husband has earned my respect. But if, on the other hand, she is frustrated and nervous and insecure, I have to conclude that there is some area of failure in the husband.

This relationship of the wife to her husband as his glory is beautifully illustrated by a "parable" from the heavenly bodies: the relationship of the moon to the sun. The moon is the "glory" of the sun. The moon has no glory of its own. Its only beauty comes from reflecting the radiance of the sun.

Some years ago, in the NASA center in Houston, Texas, I had the opportunity to see the fragment of rock from the moon's surface that had been brought back to earth by the astronauts. For a while I gazed at it in awe. Finally I bowed my head in reverent worship of the Creator as I began to understand the perfect wisdom of His design. That moon rock is dull and unattractive in itself. It has no brilliance or radiance of its own. Yet it is the most highly reflective material that man has yet discovered. Why? The reason, of course, is that it was designed by the Creator for one supreme purpose — to reflect the radiance of the sun. This it will continue to do, so long as nothing comes between it and the sun. But if some other body — for example, the earth — comes between the moon and the sun, the result is manifested in the moon. It loses its light.

All this is a parable that illustrates a much more wonderful work of the Creator's genius — the marriage relationship. The wife is like the moon. She has no glory of her own. Her function is to reflect her husband. When he shines on her, she glows. But if the full, open fellowship between them is broken — if something comes in between — the result is manifested in the wife. She loses her light.

Those of us who are husbands would do well to check from time to time on our performance in this regard. We should be ready to see our wife's condition as a reflection of our own. We males are often quick to notice some area of weakness in our wives — even perhaps to be unkind or critical about it. Yet it may well be that the problem we see so clearly in our wife is, in reality, but the reflection of a corresponding problem which has gone unrecognized in ourselves.

What should a husband look for in his wife? What should he accept as evidence that he is fulfilling his responsibility toward her? If I had to answer this question in one word, the word I would choose would be *security*. When a married woman is truly secure — emotionally secure, financially secure, socially secure — in most cases that is sufficient evidence that her relationship with her husband is good and that he is fulfilling his obligations toward her. But if a married woman is subject to frequent or continuing insecurity, almost invariably this can be traced to one of two causes: either her husband is not fulfilling his obligation to her, or something has come in between them which prevents the wife from receiving what her husband has to give her.

What are the main practical ways in which a husband should fulfill his responsibility toward his wife? I would suggest that they can be summed up in two words: to *protect* and to *provide*.

A husband's primary practical responsibility is to protect his wife. She should feel secure. She should know that she has a covering. It is unfair to ask women to take many of the responsibilities that are thrust upon them today. They may prove to be very efficient, they may even outdo men. But they lose their femininity. In most cases, the true, underlying cause is that the husband has abdicated from his responsibility to protect his wife. A wife should always know that she has someone to stand between her and every blow, every attack, every pressure.

A husband's second practical responsibility is to provide for his wife. Scripture is very clear about this. "But if anyone does not provide for his own, and especially for those of his household, he has denied the faith, and is worse than an unbeliever" (1 Timothy 5:8). The word "provide" has a wide application. A husband should see that there is no area of need in his wife for which he has not made provision — whether the need be physical, or emotional, or cultural, or spiritual.

However, one major area in which a husband is responsible to provide for his wife is that of finance. Normally, he should accept full responsibility for her financial needs. A man who does not do this when he can will almost inevitably forfeit some measure of authority in his home. It is hard to separate the earning of money from the right to make decisions about the way the money is spent. But the making of such decisions should be a function of headship. If a wife earns as much as, or more than, her husband, it is hard for him to retain effective headship.

We know, of course, that there are

exceptions to this. There are husbands who become incapacitated and unable to work. In such cases, the responsibility for financial provision may fall upon the wife. The marriage vow makes allowance for such cases as this; it covers "in sickness" as well as "in health." However, it is wrong when unfortunate exceptions such as this become the normal rule.

Briefly, now, we may sum up the mutual responsibilities of husband and wife in this covenant relationship of marriage. The main responsibilities of the husband are to *protect* and to *provide*. The main responsibilities of the wife are to *uphold* and to *encourage*. However, the proper fulfillment of these responsibilities can never be achieved by mere unaided human effort or will power. It takes something more than that, it takes the supernatural, all-sufficient grace of God. This kind of grace comes only as husband and wife together commit themselves to God and to one another in solemn, covenant relationship. It is the act of commitment that releases God's grace.

The outcome of this commitment is a new kind of life and relationship, one which can never be experienced by those who have not first met the conditions. We will go on now to see what is the distinctive character of this new life.

Union Leads to Knowing

The result of covenant commitment between a man and a woman can be summed up in one word — to KNOW. A man and a woman come to *know* each other in a depth and a degree which is not possible in any other way. The verb to "know" in the original language of Scripture has a meaning both wider and deeper than its English counterpart. In Genesis 4:1 it says, "And Adam knew Eve his wife; and she conceived, and bare Cain . . . " (This is the King James Version. The New American Standard Bible says, "the man had relations with his wife Eve." However, the King James retains the correct, literal meaning of the original Hebrew.) This is the first time that the word "know" is used in Scripture after the fall. It is also the first recorded occasion that a man and a woman came together in sexual union.

However, the writers of the Old Testament are very precise and discriminating in the way in which they use the verb to "know" to describe sexual intercourse between a man and a woman. Wherever a man came together with a woman in a covenant union which had the seal of God's approval, Scripture says that he "knew" her. But where it was an illicit relationship, one which God had not endorsed and did not approve,

Scripture says that he "lay with" her. The implication is that it is possible for a man to have sexual intercourse with a woman and yet not to "know" her. I believe that this is fully borne out in experience. Indeed, a man may have promiscuous sexual intercourse with fifty women, and yet never "know" one of them.

What, then, is the essential difference between merely "lying with" a woman and "knowing" a woman? The answer can be given in one word: *commitment.* The essence of sexual immorality is that a man and a woman seek physical and emotional satisfaction from each other, but they have not made a permanent commitment to each other. The pleasure that they obtain in this way is "stolen." They have not paid the due price for it.

This brings out how much importance God attaches to commitment. Sexual intercourse that is not preceded by permanent, mutual commitment is immorality. "Premarital sex" is the fancy title given to it in contemporary society. "Fornication" is the blunt word used in Scripture. On the other hand, sexual union that is preceded by legitimate, mutual commitment is "marriage." The difference in God's attitude toward these two relationships is clearly brought out in Hebrews 13:4: *"Let* marriage *be held* in honor among all, and *let* the *mar-*

riage bed *be* undefiled; for fornicators and adulterers God will judge." In this context, "fornicators" are to be understood as those who indulge in sexual relationships without covenant commitment. "Adulterers" are those who have made a marriage commitment, but then indulge in sexual relationships that violate their commitment. In both cases, the essence of the sin is a wrong attitude toward covenant commitment.

We return to God's ultimate purpose for marriage: that a man and a woman come to "know" each other. I suppose that the full depth of this truth can only be appreciated by those who have been privileged to experience it. Such "knowledge" between a man and a woman is neither temporary nor static. It is not merely intellectual, as we normally understand knowledge in contemporary terminology. Nor is it merely sexual. It is a total, unreserved opening up of each personality to the other. It embraces every area — physical, emotional, intellectual and spiritual. If the marriage pursues its God-ordained course, the mutual knowledge of husband and wife will become fuller and deeper as the years pass.

It is my personal conviction that the greatest wonder of all God's creative achievement is expressed in human personality. Jesus taught that one human soul is worth more than the whole world (Mark 8:36—37). I believe this is a true, objective evaluation. The whole created universe, in all its grandeur and greatness, is of less intrinsic worth than one human personality. The marvel of marriage is that, through it, two human personalities are permitted to know each other in all their uniqueness, permitted to explore the sacred, innermost depths of each other. But just because marriage in this sense is so wondrous and so sacred, God has protected it with His demand for covenant commitment.

There are countless different facets to the way in which a man and his wife may come to know one another. For instance, the very way in which they look at one another is different from the way in which they look at other people, or other people look at them. One of my favorite (but unclassified) occupations is watching a husband and wife when they are not aware that anyone is watching them. What I always look at is their eyes. (Someone has said that the eye is the "window of the soul.") Give me time to observe the looks that a husband and wife exchange between themselves, and I will form a pretty accurate estimate of how successful their marriage is.

A wife has a way of looking at her husband that tells him almost everything without saying anything in words. For instance, "It's time you took care of the kids." Or, "You shouldn't have spent so long talking to that other woman." Or, "If we go home now, we can have an hour together by ourselves." For this reason, Scripture indicates that a married woman should never permit herself to look at any other person in the way that she looks at her husband.

This is very vividly illustrated by an incident in the life of Abraham. Abraham was a great man of faith, but he had certain very human weaknesses. On two occasions, in order to save his own life, he was prepared to let his wife Sarah be taken into the harem of a Gentile king. He was slow to realize that divine destiny had linked him irrevocably with Sarah, and could never be fulfilled through any other woman. Abraham's weakness in this respect should serve as a warning to husbands in this age. In 1 Peter 3:7, Christian husbands are reminded that their wife is, with them, "a fellow-heir of the grace of life." The phrase "fellow-heir" indicates a joint inheritance, one which neither party can legally claim apart from the other. There are areas of God's inheritance for married couples which neither can enter without the other. These areas are reserved solely for couples who can move together in mutual love and harmony. This principle applies as much to Christian husbands today as it did in Abraham's relationship to Sarah.

The second of the two occasions on which Abraham was prepared to part with Sarah was in the court of Abimelech, king of Gerar (see Genesis chapter 20). Abraham persuaded Sarah to say that she was his sister — which was true, but not the whole truth — and to conceal the fact that she was also his wife. As a result, Abimelech took her into his harem, intending to make her his wife. However, God intervened supernaturally to preserve Sarah. In a dream, He revealed to Abimelech that Sarah was really Abraham's wife, and warned him that if he took her, he would pay for it with his own life. Abimelech, who was apparently a God-fearing man, immediately returned Sarah to Abraham and compensated him with substantial gifts for the wrong that he had done.

In conclusion, however, Abimelech addresses a word of reproof and warning to Sarah: "And unto Sarah he said, Behold, I have given thy brother a thousand *pieces* of silver: behold, he *is* to thee a covering of the eyes, unto all that *are* with thee, and with all *other:* thus she was reproved" (Genesis 20:16 KJV). We may sum up the essence of Abimelech's reproof to Sarah in this way: "When you are married, you may never look at another man in the way that you look at your husband. He is a covering of the eyes to you." There is a way in which a woman opens up her eyes to her husband that is both scriptural and very sacred. She should never deliberately let any other man look into her eyes the way her husband does.

Obviously, there is another side to this. Just as a married woman has no right to look in this way at a man who is not her husband; so a married man has no right to *receive* such a look from a woman who is not his wife. To his credit, it would seem that Abimelech recognized this.

At any rate, this warning given to Sarah by Abimelech expresses in a simple, but vivid way, the essence of the relationship into which a man and woman enter through the covenant of marriage. Through their covenant commitment to each other, they come to know one another in a way in which neither of them should ever know any other person and no other person should ever know either of them. The purpose of the marriage covenant is to preserve this unique and sacred knowledge between husband and wife, and to keep it from being violated by any other relationship.

4

UNION WITH GOD

The marriage covenant is not merely sacred in its own right. It is sacred also because it typifies other relationships of great spiritual significance. The first and the most important of these is the relationship that God desires to have with His people.

God: the Husband
of His People

In various passages of the Old Testament God compares His relationship with Israel to that of a husband with a wife. He traces this relationship back to the covenant that He made with Israel at Mount Sinai, after He had delivered them out of Egypt. Thus God's relationship as a husband to Israel, like the human relationship of a man with his wife, is based on a covenant that He entered into when He made them His people. This is clearly brought out in Jeremiah 31:31—32:

(31) "Behold, days are coming," de-

clares the LORD, "when I will make a new covenant with the house of Israel and with the house of Judah,
(32)   not like the covenant which I made with their fathers in the day I took them by the hand to bring them out of the land of Egypt, My covenant which they broke, although I was a husband to them," declares the LORD.

God says here that when He brought Israel out of Egypt and made a covenant with them, by that act He entered into the relationship of a husband to them. However, by unfaithfulness and idolatry, Israel violated their covenant and forfeited their right to this relationship with God as their husband. Nevertheless, rather than finally rejecting Israel for their unfaithfulness, God here declares that, at the close of this age, He will make a new covenant with them, and thus once again become their husband.

In Hosea 3:1 we again find God's relationship with Israel pictured as that of a husband to his wife: "Then the LORD said to me, 'Go, again love a woman *who* is loved by *her* husband, yet an adulteress, even as the LORD loves the sons of Israel, though they turn to other gods and love raisin cakes." By his continuing love for his wife Gomer, in spite of her unfaithfulness, the prophet Hosea becomes a type of God's continuing love for Israel, as their husband, which does not cease even though they have been persistently unfaithful on their side of the relationship.

In Hosea, as in Jeremiah, there is a prophetic promise that God will eventually bring Israel back into covenant with Himself, and thereby restore His relationship to them as their husband. In Hosea 2:16, He declares:
"And it will come about in that day," declares the LORD,
"That you will call Me Ishi (i.e. my Husband) And will no longer call Me Baali (i.e. my Master)."

Then, in Hosea 2:18 He speaks of the new covenant that He will make with them; and in verses 19 and 20 He pictures the result of this covenant as the restoration of His marriage relationship to them:

   (19)   "And I will betroth you to Me forever;
        Yes, I will betroth you to Me in righteousness and in justice,
        In lovingkindness and in compassion,
   (20)   And I will betroth you to Me in faithfulness.
        Then you will know the LORD."

There is special significance in the closing statement of verse 20: "Then you will know the LORD." We have already seen that, in the

70

natural, covenant brings a man and a woman into a union in which they come to know each other as they never could without such a commitment. Here the principle is applied to Israel's restored relationship to God. Through their covenant commitment they will come to "know the Lord" as they have never known Him before.

Briefly, then, we may sum up the Old Testament picture of God's relationship to Israel as follows: The covenant which God made with Israel at Mount Sinai is viewed as establishing a marriage relationship between God and Israel, through which He became their husband. Subsequently, through unfaithfulness and idolatry, Israel violated the covenant and forfeited their right to this relationship. God did not finally reject Israel on this account, nor did His love for them cease. Therefore, His ultimate purpose is to establish a new covenant with them, through which He will once again enter into the relationship of a husband to them. This new covenant, unlike the first, will be eternal. It will never be violated. Through it, Israel will come to know the Lord with a totally new depth of intimacy, such as they have never hitherto experienced.

The New Testament more fully unveils the nature of this new covenant. It will be based not on the sacrifice of animals, but on the atoning death of Jesus Christ, the

Son of God. This is the covenant into which all those of whatever race or background who acknowledge Jesus as Savior and Lord, have already entered. Consistent with the pattern already established in the Old Testament, this new covenant in Christ is viewed as bringing believers into a relationship with God which is analogous to the marriage relationship between husband and wife.

In Ephesians 5:25—33 Paul says that Christ redeems and sanctifies His church in order that He may present it to Himself as a bride is presented to her husband, "holy and blameless." Paul goes on to apply this truth in a practical way to the natural relationship between husband and wife, but he closes by saying: "This mystery is great; but I am speaking with reference to Christ and the church." In other words, the relationship between Christ and the church is analogous to that between a husband and his wife.

One Spirit with God

In 1 Corinthians 6:16—17 Paul applies this picture not merely to the relationship of God to His people as a whole, but also to the relationship that God desires to have with each individual believer:

(16) Or do you not know that the one

who joins himself to a harlot is one body *with her?* For He Says, "THE TWO WILL BECOME ONE FLESH."

(17) But the one who joins himself to Lord is one spirit *with Him.*

As usual with the writers of Scripture, Paul is very frank. He is speaking about sexual union between a man and a woman. He says that a man who has sexual union with a harlot makes himself one body with her. Then he goes on to say that a believer can have a similar kind of union with God in which he becomes one spirit with God. Thus, the relationship that God invites each believer to have with Him is precisely parallel, on the spiritual plane, to the sexual union which, on the physical plane, a man may have with a woman.

In our previous chapter we have already seen the essential difference between the marriage union, which is pure and holy, and fornication, which is sinful. The difference is that the marriage union is preceded by mutual covenant commitment on the part of the man and the woman. In fornication, on the other hand, a man and a woman seek sexual satisfaction from each other, without being willing to make a covenant commitment to each other.

The language Paul uses in 1 Corinthians 6:16—17 clearly justifies us in applying this principle also to the relationship between God and the believer. God desires spiritual union with each believer. At the same time, however, it is certain that God will never violate His own laws. He will never be a party to spiritual "fornication." Therefore, union with God in this sense depends upon, and must be preceded by, covenant commitment to God. Until a believer is ready to make the total unreserved commitment to God which covenant requires, he can never have this full spiritual union with God which is the purpose of redemption.

Earlier, in examining Psalm 50:5, we saw how God defines His "godly ones." They are those "who cut a covenant with Him on the basis of a sacrifice." The lesson is the same as that of 1 Corinthians 6:16—17. There is no way to the intimacy of union with God, which is godliness, except through covenant commitment. Without such commitment, a person can never truly be a "godly one." He can never be truly united with God.

This explains the pathetic condition of many people in our churches today. They desire a relationship with God. They may even lay claim to such a relationship. Nevertheless, their desire is unfulfilled; their claim is unjustified. The reason: they have never made that solemn, unreserved, personal commitment to God which is the only basis upon which He will receive them into the relationship that they desire.

Such persons may indeed have "made a decision" at an evangelistic campaign. Or they may have gone forward in a church and shaken the pastor by the hand. Or they may have gone through a religious ritual, such as baptism or confirmation. But all these acts — and many others too numerous to list — are of no avail, unless they bring people into a vital, committed, covenant relationship with God. Short of this, there can be no true intimacy with God. He does not commit Himself to the uncommitted.

Life's Purpose is Knowing God

For those, however, who are willing to enter into this type of covenant commitment to God, the reward is great. It is beautifully expressed by the words which Jesus addresses to the Father in John 17:3: "And this is eternal life, that they may know Thee the only true God, and Jesus Christ, whom Thou hast sent." I once heard a paraphrase which rendered this, "And this is the *purpose of eternal life*, that they may know Thee, the only true God . . . " Here, indeed, is the ultimate purpose of all life — to know the one true God. Out of this knowledge there comes eternal life — divine life — the life of God Himself, shared with the believer.

However, "knowledge" of this kind is not merely intellectual. It is not merely theology, or doctrine. It is not *knowing about* God. It is actually knowing God Himself — knowing Him directly and intimately — knowing Him as a Person. It is a person-to-person relationship. It is a spiritual union.

Knowing God in this way is exactly parallel, on the spiritual plane, to the way in which a man may come to "know" a woman as his wife, and a woman may come to "know" a man as her husband. The use in Scripture of the same word to describe each type of relationship is no accident. It reveals the deep underlying similarity that exists between the two relationships. In the natural, a man and a woman can never truly "know" one another, unless they first make an unreserved, covenant commitment to each other. In the spiritual, a believer can never truly "know" God unless he has first made an unreserved, covenant commitment to God. The same principle applies on each plane: without covenant there can be no union; and without commitment there can be no covenant.

Does commitment of this kind sound too intense for you? Too intimate? Too absolute? In the last resort, each of us must make his own decision about this. But let me say that, for my part, I am not interested in some watered-down, religious substitute for the real thing. Rather I echo the words of David in Psalm 63:1:

O God, Thou art my God; I shall seek Thee
earnestly;
My soul thirsts for Thee, my flesh yearns
for Thee,
In a dry and weary land where there is no
water.

To the soul that is truly thirsty, there can
be only one source of ultimate satisfaction:
it is God Himself. To stop at less than true
union with Him is to miss the real purpose of
living. It is to remain forever frustrated, forever unfulfilled.

In Isaiah 1:22 God tells rebellious, backslidden Israel, "Your silver has become dross,
your drink diluted with water." The same
could be said to many churches today. Everything has lost its purity, its true character.
We are asked to accept something adulterated
and impure, a counterfeit of the real thing.

In the natural, if somebody were to offer
me wine diluted with water, my response
would be, "Spare yourself the trouble, keep
the whole thing!" But today in the church
and in society we are mixing everything with
water. We dilute it, we water it down, we
lower the standards. Our silver no longer has
its proper value; our wine no longer has its
proper flavor.

In such a spiritual climate, it takes a
person of considerable strength of character
to settle for nothing less than God's best.

Such a person must be willing to say: "Others may do it the way they please, I will do it God's way. I want a real relationship with God. I want a marriage that works, a home that glorifies God, children that grow up happy and secure. Yes, I want these things — and I am willing to pay the price!"

God has made the price quite clear: it is a covenant commitment — on the vertical plane, to God Himself — on the horizontal plane, to our mate.

5

UNION WITH GOD'S PEOPLE

In our two preceding chapters we have seen that covenant is the indispensable condition for true union. In chapter 3, we saw how this principle applies to the union between a man and a woman, which we call marriage. In chapter 4, we saw how it applies also to the union of each believer with God, which on the spiritual plane is analogous to the marriage union between a man and a woman. In this chapter, we will examine how the same principle applies to yet another relationship of vital importance: that is, the relationship of God's people, one to another.

Covenant Makes a "People"

In the Old Testament we find that from the time God entered into a covenant with Abraham, his descendants (through the line of Isaac and Jacob) were set apart from all other members of the human race. Thenceforth they were known as "the seed of Abraham." However, the out-working of

God's purpose required that the covenant be established a second time, not with Abraham individually, but with all his descendants collectively. This took place at Mount Sinai, after the Exodus. Thereafter they were designated by a new title in the singular form: "a people" (Hebrew *'am*). This indicated that, through entering into the covenant, they had become a new, collective unit.

The process by which God entered into His covenant with Israel is described in Exodus chapter 19 and following. In Exodus 19:5—6 God declares the purpose for which He is bringing Israel into covenant relationship with Himself.

> (5) 'Now then, if you will indeed obey My voice and keep My covenant, then you shall be My own possession among all the peoples, for all the earth is Mine:
> (6) and you shall be to Me a kingdom of priests and a holy nation.' . . .

We need to understand that Israel was thenceforth set apart to God as a special people, not by any intrinsic righteousness of their own, but by the covenant God made with them. It is important to see that their holiness was the *outcome* of the covenant, not the *reason* for it. To express this another way: God did not enter into a covenant with

Israel because they were holy; rather, He made them holy by entering into a covenant with them.

In our preceding chapter, we saw that, on the basis of this covenant, God assumed toward them the relationship and the responsibility of a husband. The covenant established a relationship between God and Israel analogous to that between a husband and a wife. It gave them a unique relationship to God in the same way that marriage gives a woman a unique relationship to her husband.

However, the only basis on which Israel had a right to continue in this unique and special relationship with God was by continuing faithful to the covenant. For this reason, God prefixed the declaration of His purpose for them by the word "if." "*If* you will obey My voice and keep My covenant, then you shall be my own possession among all the peoples . . . and a holy nation." Israel's continuing unique relationship to God was, therefore, bound up with their abiding by the terms of the covenant. For this reason, when Israel later lapsed into idolatry, their prophets frequently categorized their sin as "adultery." It was analogous to that of a wife who had failed to abide by her marriage commitment to her husband.

From the time that God established

this covenant with Israel, the Hebrew usage of the Old Testament maintains a careful distinction between two related Hebrew words: *goy* ("nation") and *'am* ("people"). All nations, including Israel, are *goyim* (plural of *goy*) — "nations." But Israel alone is also *'am* — a "people." That which singles Israel out by this distinctive title from all other nations is their unique covenant relationship with God.

In the New Testament the same distinction is maintained by the use of two different Greek words: *ethnos* ("nation" — corresponding to the Hebrew *goy*) and *laos* ("people" — corresponding to the Hebrew *'am*). The Greek *ethnos*, in its plural form *ethne*, is translated alternatively "nations" or "gentiles." It is important to understand that the word "gentiles" normally refers not to people who are not Christians, but to people who are not Israelites.

This analysis of the distinctive words used both in Hebrew and in Greek for "people" and "nation" has been necessary to establish one vital basic principle of Scripture: it takes a *covenant* (*b'rit*) to constitute a *people* (*'am*). An ethnic group that has no collective covenant with God is merely a "nation," but an ethnic group that has a collective covenant with God is, by that fact, a "people."

Covenant Relationships:
Vertical and Horizontal

If we turn back once more to the passage in Exodus chapter 19 and following, where God enters into a covenant with Israel, we discover a second, related principle: the same covenant that brought Israel into a unique relationship with God also, by that fact, brought them into a unique relationship with one another. The main purpose of the following chapters of Exodus — chapters 20 through 23 — is to define the specific, practical ways in which God required them, from then onward, to relate to one another. As members of one covenant people, they had special obligations to each other, different from those which they had to members of other nations who had no covenant relationship either with God or with Israel.

We may state this principle more generally, as follows: those who have a covenant relationship with God necessarily also have a covenant relationship with each other. The relationships established by a covenant are in two directions — vertical and horizontal. The covenant that brings us into union vertically with God must of necessity also bring us into union horizontally with all who have entered into the same covenant with God. We have no right to claim the benefits of covenant relationship with God, while at the same time refusing to accept our obligations toward those who share the same covenant with Him. The same covenant that brings individuals into union with God also brings them into collective union with one another. It establishes them collectively as a "people" — set apart from all other collective units of humanity.

These principles concerning covenant, established in the Old Testament, are carried over, unchanged, into the New Testament. When Jesus celebrated the last supper with His disciples, and shared with them the bread and the wine, by that act He brought them into a covenant relationship with Himself. After He had handed them the cup and told them all to drink of it, He said, "This is My blood of the covenant" (Matthew 26:28). They not merely shared the cup of the covenant with Him; they also shared it with each other. The same solemn act that brought each of them into covenant with Jesus at the same time brought them all into covenant with one another. Thenceforth, their covenant relationship was not merely vertical, to Jesus; it was also horizontal, to each other.

This is borne out by 1 Corinthians 10:16—17, where Paul is explaining the significance of the Lord's supper. He emphasizes this horizontal relationship between all who partake of the one loaf and the one cup:

(16) Is not the cup of blessing which we bless a sharing in the blood of Christ? Is not the bread which we break a sharing in the body of Christ?

(17) Since there is one bread, we who are many are one body; for we all partake of the one bread.

In 1 Peter 2:9—10, Peter declares that the new covenant in Christ has the same effect as God's previous covenant with Israel: it establishes all who enter into it as a collective "people."

(9) But you are A CHOSEN RACE, A ROYAL PRIESTHOOD, A HOLY NATION, A PEOPLE FOR *God's* OWN POSSESSION, that you may proclaim the excellencies of Him who has called you out of darkness into His marvelous light; [Peter is quoting the very words spoken by God to Israel in Exodus 19:5—6]

(10) for you once were NOT A PEOPLE, but now you are THE PEOPLE OF GOD; you had NOT RECEIVED MERCY, but now you have RECEIVED MERCY.

We have already seen in two cases that

the end purpose of covenant is *union*. The purpose of the marriage covenant is to bring a man and a woman into union with each other. The purpose of the covenant between God and the individual believer is to bring the believer into union with God. This principle applies with equal force to the third case — the covenant between believers. Its purpose is to bring all believers into union with each other

After Jesus had shared the bread and wine of the New Covenant with His disciples, He went on to share with them the long and intimate discourse recorded in John chapters 14, 15 and 16. This discourse came to its climax with His "high-priestly" prayer for them, recorded in John chapter 17. This prayer, in turn, comes to its climax with His plea to the Father that all who believe in Him "may be one, just as We are one" (John 17:22). In this context, we understand that this plea constitutes the outworking of the covenant which He had established with them earlier that evening. The end purpose of the covenant is union — of the same nature and quality as that which exists between the Father and the Son. Until we, as believers, have come into this unity, we have not fulfilled our covenant obligations — either to Christ or to one another.

We have already pointed out that when God made His covenant with Israel at Mount

Sinai, He immediately went on to explain to the Israelites the obligations which the covenant would impose upon them in their relationships and dealings with one another. These obligations are set out — in specific and practical terms — in Exodus chapters 20 through 23. In a corresponding way, the New Testament sets forth, for all who enter into the New Covenant in Christ, the ways in which they are obligated, by their covenant commitment, to relate to one another. It is outside the scope of this book to examine in detail all the mutual obligations of believers toward each other. However, we may form a general picture of these obligations by simply picking out phrases such as "each other" or "one to another" wherever they occur in the New Testament and listing the various mutual obligations which are thereby indicated.

All who have entered into the New Covenant in Christ are required to behave in the following ways toward one another:

to WASH one another's FEET (John 13:14)

to LOVE one another (John 13:14, et al)

to BUILD UP one another (Romans 14:19)

to ACCEPT one another (Romans 15:7)

to ADMONISH one another (Romans 15:14, et al)

to GREET one another (Romans 16:16, et al)

to SERVE one another (Galatians 5:13)

to BEAR one another's BURDENS (Galatians 6:2)

to SHOW FORBEARANCE to one another (Ephesians 4:2)

to FORGIVE one another (Ephesians 4:32)

to BE SUBJECT to one another (Ephesians 5:21)

to TEACH one another (Colossians 3:16)

to COMFORT one another (1 Thessalonians 4:18)

to ENCOURAGE one another (Hebrews 3:13)

to STIMULATE one another to LOVE and GOOD DEEDS (Hebrews 10:24)

to CONFESS their SINS to one another (James 5:16)

to PRAY for one another (James 5:16)

to BE HOSPITABLE to one another (1 Peter 4:9)

to BE CLOTHED WITH HUMILITY toward one another (1 Peter 5:5)

Only insofar as we, as believers, discharge these mutual responsibilities toward one another, are we fulfilling the terms of the New Covenant.

Although the obligations of the New Covenant are stated in a somewhat different form from those of the covenant made at

Mount Sinai, the basic principle is the same in both: those who enter into a covenant with God are — by that very act — necessarily brought into covenant with one another. The obligations of each such covenant extend in two directions: vertically, between the covenant people and God; horizontally, between the members of the covenant people.

Only Death Makes
The Covenant Valid

Another principle which applies equally in each covenant is that it is valid only on the basis of the sacrifice. This general principle is stated, as we saw in chapter 2, in Hebrews 9:16—17:

(16)　For where a covenant is, there must of necessity be the death of the one who made it.

(17)　For a covenant is valid *only* when men are dead, for it is never in force while the one who made it lives.

In the next three verses, the writer of Hebrews applies this principle specifically to the covenant between God and Israel which was mediated by Moses at Mount Sinai:

(18)　Therefore even the first *covenant* was not inaugurated without blood.

(19) For when every commandment had been spoken by Moses to all the people according to the Law, he took the blood of the calves and the goats, with water and scarlet wool and hyssop, and sprinkled both the book itself and all the people,

(20) saying, "THIS IS THE BLOOD OF THE COVENANT WHICH GOD COMMANDED YOU."

In each case, the death of the sacrifice represented the death of those who entered by it into the covenant. The animals sacrificed by Moses merely reminded Israel of the principle that covenant was valid only through death, and prefigured a different kind of sacrifice that had not yet been offered. On the other hand, the death of Jesus on the cross was *substitutionary*. He died as the personal representative of all who were to enter into the covenant with God through Him. Jesus identified Himself with each in death, that each in turn might identify himself with Jesus. As this two-way identification is worked out through the ongoing commitment of each believer, the death of Jesus becomes, effectively and experientially, the death of the believer. This principle is clearly stated by Paul in 2 Corinthians 5:14—15:

(14) For the love of Christ controls us,

having concluded this, that one died for all, therefore all died;

(15) and He died for all, that they who live should no longer live for themselves, but for Him who died and rose again on their behalf.

Paul's conclusion is both clear and logical. It is summed up in the words, *"therefore all died."* If we accept Christ's death as our death, then we must "consider ourselves to be dead" (Romans 6:11). Therefore we are no longer free to live for ourselves. This, too, has a two-way application: vertically, toward the Lord; horizontally, toward the Lord's people. When the Lord and Abram entered into covenant with each other, each voluntarily abrogated the right to live only for himself. Each, by the "cutting" of the covenant, said, in effect, to the other: "That is my death . . . As I enter into this covenant, I enter by death. Now that I am in covenant, I have no more right to live."

The same relationship that was established, person-to-person, between the Lord and Abram on that memorable night is re-established between all who, through the death of Jesus, are brought into covenant with each other. Each of us reaffirms the mutual covenant of which the Lord and Abram are the prototype, the original pattern. Each says to the other: "That is my death. As I enter into this covenant, I enter by death. Now that I am in covenant, I have no more right to live.''

In 1 John 3:16—17 the outworking of the death which alone makes our covenant valid is applied by the apostle specifically to our relationship with our fellow believers:

(16) We know love by this, that He laid down His life for us; and we ought to lay down our lives for the brethren.

(17) But whoever has the world's goods, and beholds his brother in need and closes his heart against him, how does the love of God abide in him?

The phrase ''we ought to'' expresses an obligation — one which we cannot evade if we claim to be partakers of the same covenant. When John speaks about ''laying down our lives,'' he is not speaking solely — or even primarily — about undergoing physical death. He makes this quite clear, because in the next verse he applies it to making our ''worldly goods'' available to our fellow believers. If we are not willing to do this, where there is a legitimate need, then we are not willing to ''lay down our lives.'' ''Laying down our lives'' means being ready to share with our covenant brothers and sisters both what we are and what we have. If we are not willing to do this, our covenant commitment is not genuine.

The New Life Style —
Koinonia

In the Greek vocabulary of the New Testament there is one very important word which describes the distinctive life style into which we are initiated through the New Covenant. It is *koinonia*. The noun *koinonia* is derived from the adjective *koinos* — "common." Literally and basically, *koinonia* is "having in common." Insofar as two or more persons have things in common, they have *koinonia*. If there are any areas where they do not have things in common, in those areas they do not have *koinonia*. It was said of the early church in Jerusalem, "all things were *common property* to them" (Acts 4:32). That was *koinonia*.

In the majority of English translations of the New Testament, *koinonia* is translated "fellowship." However, in some versions it is not translated by a single English word, but by a phrase, such as "to be in union with," or "to share in common life." Because there is no one English word which fully expresses its meanings, in this chapter we will continue to use the word in its Greek form — *koinonia*.

Koinonia is the outworking of true unity. The perfect example of *koinonia* is the relationship between God the Father and God the Son. In John 10:30, Jesus says, "I and the Father are one." This unity between the Father and the Son is the basis of their *koinonia*. Its outworking is described by Jesus in John 16:14—15, where He says of the Holy Spirit, "He shall take of Mine, and disclose *it* to you." But then He immediately explains, "All things that the Father has are Mine . . . " In other words, Jesus says, "All that is Mine I have not in my own right, but on the basis of My unity with the Father."

In John 17:10, Jesus states the same again in His prayer to the Father: "All things that are Mine are Thine, and Thine are Mine . . . " This is perfect *koinonia* — the having of all things in common.

In this sense, the gospel is an invitation from the Father and the Son to all members of the human race to share with them the perfect *koinonia* that they share with each other. In 1 Corinthians 1:9, Paul says, "God is faithful, through whom you were called into fellowship (*koinonia*) with His Son, Jesus Christ our Lord." It is important to distinguish between "means" and "ends." So many forms of religious activity are "means" rather than "ends." They are not valuable in themselves, but only insofar as they enable us to achieve "ends," which alone are valuable in themselves. *Koinonia,* however, is not a mere "means;" it is an "end." It is, in fact, the supreme end of all worthwhile religious activity.

In 1 John 1:3—4, John likewise declares that the end purpose of the gospel is to bring all who respond into the same eternal *koinonia* which the Father and the Son enjoy between themselves:

(3)   What we have seen and heard we proclaim to you also, that you also may have fellowship *(koinonia)* with us; and indeed our fellowship *(koinonia)* is with the Father, and with His Son Jesus Christ.

(4)   And these things we write, so that our joy may be made complete.

"What we have seen and heard" is the eyewitness testimony of Christ's apostles, preserved for us in the pages of the New Testament. These verses, therefore, disclose the central purpose for which God caused the gospel record to be preserved and transmitted. It is that all who believe and obey may have opportunity to share in the perfect, eternal *koinonia*, which is the life style of heaven.

The Price of *Koinonia*

However, *koinonia* is not cheap. There is a price to pay. It is set by two unvarying requirements. The first is *commitment*; the second is a way of life that is called "*walking in the light.*"

Covenant, as we have seen, is the door to unity. Only those who are willing to make the total, unreserved commitment of a covenant can ever come into true unity with each other. This applies alike in the relationship between husband and wife; between the believer and God; and between believers in fellowship together.

Thereafter this commitment is worked out through "walking in the light." In 1 John 1:7, John says, "But if we walk in the light as He Himself is in the light, we have fellowship *(koinonia)* with one another . . ." "Walking in the light" is the only way to experience *koinonia*. Wherever Scripture speaks of *koinonia*, it acknowledges only one standard — that of God Himself. It is expressed here by the phrase, "as He Himself is in the light." God is willing to lift humanity up to His own level of *koinonia,* but He is not willing to lower the standard of *koinonia* to that of unredeemed humanity — or even of backslidden Christendom.

At the same time, the phrase "in the light" sets boundaries to what may be shared in *koinonia.* Anything that contravenes divine law in the realm of morals or ethics is not "in the light." On the contrary, it is darkness. An obvious example is in the area of sexual relationship. It is in accordance with divine law for a husband and wife to have sexual relationship with each other. This is fully "in the light." But for either of them to have sexual relationship with any other person is contrary to divine law. It is no longer "in the light."

Subject to this reservation, however, "walking in the light" is a relationship of total, continuing honesty and openness between all who are in *koinonia*. Nothing may be hidden, or misrepresented, or held back. The essence of the relationship is the same whether it is between a husband and wife, or between a group of believers who are committed to each other. We may sum it up in the words which we used in chapter 3 to describe the husband-wife relationship: a total, unreserved opening up of each personality to the others.

Thus the limits of *koinonia* are governed by two factors: divine law and absolute honesty. Divine law sets the boundaries; whatever contravenes divine law is no longer *koinonia*. It is darkness, not light. But within those boundaries, the light must be full and unrestricted. Wherever dishonesty, or insincerity, or selfish reservations creep in, the light begins to dim. *Koinonia* is no longer on the divine level.

What shall we say of Christians who seek fellowship one with another, but are not willing to meet these requirements? Logically, we must say the same as we would of a man and a woman who seek a sexual relationship, but are not willing to meet the requirements for marriage. The result which they achieve is not *koinonia*, but "fornication." This is equally true whether it be on the physical plane between a man and a woman, or on the spiritual plane between Christians who seek a permanent relationship with each other. Those who refuse God's requirements are, by His standards, guilty of fornication. That there is such a thing as spiritual fornications is attested by the Old Testament, whose prophets charged Israel with this very sin time and time again.

The results of such wrong, uncommitted relationships between Christians in a group are very similar to those that develop between a man and a woman in a wrong sexual relationship. They are: hurt, bitterness, strife, broken relationships, unfulfilled promises, and unsatisfied yearnings. When we judge by results, we are compelled to acknowledge that in many sections of professing Christendom today, there is little evidence of true *koinonia*, but abundant evidence of wholesale spiritual fornication.

Our purpose in this chapter has been to set forth as clearly as possible the scriptural remedy for this tragic situation. It lies in a return to God's requirements: covenant commitment that is walked out "in the light."

6

THE POINT OF DECISION

In our preceding chapters we have dealt with three of the most important relationships there are in life. In order of priority, they are: our personal relationship with God; our relationship with our mate (if we are married); our relationship with God's believing people. In each of these areas we have seen the type of relationship which God has made available to those who will believe and obey Him.

Perhaps you have come to realize that you have been living on too low a level in one or more of these areas. You are ready to move up to a new level, but you are not sure how to do it. Let me remind you, therefore, that in every case there is one simple, but essential requirement. It is expressed by a word that we have used many times in this book: *commitment*.

Commitment to God

Let me speak first about the area of your

personal relationship with God. You may be a churchgoer, or at least have a church background. You may be familiar with the accepted phrases used by religious people. You may actually have experienced moments of uplift or inspiration when you knew that God was real.

Alternatively, you may be a person with no church background. Although you are not an adherent of any definite religion, there is a hunger in your heart which you long to satisfy.

Or again, you may not belong to either of these categories. You may have come to this moment by some unique route of your own. That really is not the issue just now. What matters is that you have come to a point where you long for an intimate, personal relationship with God — something so deep and real that you will never again need to question it. You are ready, therefore, to make a sincere, wholehearted commitment of yourself to God through Jesus Christ.

The natural way for you to make your commitment is by prayer. In this way you give expression to what is in your heart, and in the process of verbalizing it, you give it content. You make your commitment *specific*. A prayer of this kind is like crossing a bridge. It takes you over into new territory.

From this moment on you will not be relying on something vague and undefined in the shadowy realm of your mind. After praying, you will know *what* you are committed to. You will also know *when* and *where* you made your commitment. Your ongoing relationship with God will henceforth have a definite starting point — something fixed in a time-space world — *a point of decision.*

My counsel is that you put the book down right now — and pray! If you feel able to pray in your own words, then do so. But if you find that difficult, here is a prepared prayer that you may use:

God, you have put a desire in my heart to know you in a real and personal way. Even if I do not fully understand everything, I believe what the Bible says about Jesus Christ: that He took my sins upon Himself, died in my place, and rose again from the dead. In His Name I ask you now to forgive all my sins and to receive me as your child. Sincerely, and with my whole heart, I commit myself to you — all I am and all I have. Take me as I am, and make me what you want me to be. In faith, I believe you do hear this prayer, and you do receive me. I thank you. In Jesus' Name. *Amen.*

Once you have prayed your prayer of commitment, do not begin to reason or speculate. In simple faith, take God at His word. He has promised to receive you, if you come to Him through Jesus Christ. Thank Him, therefore, that He has done what He promised. Keep on thanking Him! The more you thank Him, the more your faith will grow.

From now on, make it your main aim to cultivate your new relationship with God. This will give you a simple standard by which to evaluate the various influences and activities in your life. Do they strengthen your relationship with God? Or do they weaken it? Make more and more room for the things which strengthen it; less and less for those which weaken it. Specifically, there are two ways to strengthen the relationship which are particularly important.

First, make your commitment known to those around you. You will not need to be aggressive, or to put on a "religious" air. But as opportunities come in the normal course of daily life, make it known in a quiet but firm way, that Jesus is now in full control of your life.

Second, set aside a period of each day for God. Spend part of this period reading your Bible, and part of it praying — that is, talking to God in a sincere and natural way. In this way you will maintain continuing two-way communication with God. As you read your Bible, God speaks to you. As you pray, you speak to God.

Probably you will not achieve instant "sainthood!" If you fail from time to time, do not become discouraged. Simply acknowledge your failures to God, and ask Him to forgive you. If other people are affected by your failures, you may need to ask them also for forgiveness. But do not give up! Remember, commitment is a two-way street. Not only are you committed to God; He is also committed to you. And He is omnipotent!

Commitment to Your Mate

The second area that we have dealt with — in order of priority — is your relationship to your mate — husband or wife, as the case may be. (Of course, if you are not married, and not expecting to marry, this section does not directly concern you.)

You may already have been a committed believer before you read this book. Or again, you may just have prayed a prayer of commitment after reading the previous section. But either way, you are now face to face with the fact that your marriage is not what it ought to be. Perhaps you have realized for the first time what it *could* be. You have come to understand that, for committed believers, marriage is "a cord of three strands" — a covenant between you, your mate and God. But it will take your personal commitment to make the covenant effective, and thus to release into your marriage the vital element that has hitherto been missing — the all-sufficient, supernatural grace of God.

Ideally, you and your mate should both make the commitment at the same time, to God and to each other. However, it some-times happens that one party is ready before the other. So if you are ready, but your mate is not, make your commitment now, and trust God to bring your mate to the same point that you have already reached — *the point of decision.* Then, when that hap-pens, you can renew your commitment together.

If you feel able to pray in your own words, do so. Otherwise here is a prepared prayer that you may use:

> *Father God, I come to you in the Name of Jesus, my Savior and Lord. I thank you that you redeemed me through the Blood of Jesus, and that I belong to you. I thank you for my marriage. I thank you for my mate. At this moment I want to commit myself*

104

*to you, to my marriage and to my mate.
I am ready, Lord, to lay down my life
and live it out through my mate, seeking
my mate's good before my own, rejoicing
in my mate's blessing and my mate's
success, counting it as mine, living now
in the life of my mate. Father God,
accept this commitment in the Name of
Jesus. Set the seal of your Holy Spirit
upon it. Bless our marriage and our
home in a new way from this day forward.*
                                           Amen.

In our previous section, "Commitment
to God," we recommended certain simple
steps to make that commitment effective.
For the most part, the same principles apply
to the commitment you have now made to
your mate and to your marriage.

First of all, make sure that your priorities
are right. Quite probably, this may neces-
sitate some adjustments. After your personal
relationship to God, the next most important
area of your life is your marriage and your
home. Evaluate your various activities ac-
cordingly. Make more and more room for
those which strengthen your marriage and
your home; less and less for those which
have the opposite effect.

In connection with your personal relationship with God, we pointed out the need to
set aside time to maintain two-way communi-
cations with Him. The same applies to your

relationship with your mate. Open, continuing communication between the two of you is vital. It will take time — more time, probably, than you have been giving to it. Remember, the way you allocate your time is the surest indication of your real priorities. You may say that your marriage is important to you, but if you allow disproportionate amounts of time to other activities, you are really giving them priority over your marriage.

Someone coined the saying: "The family that prays together stays together." There is a great deal of truth in it. For thirty years Lydia and I prayed and read the Bible together almost every day — usually twice a day. Often God spoke to us in a very intimate way in these times of communication with Him and with each other. They were one of the principle factors in the success of our marriage.

Sometimes, I have observed, husband and wife find it difficult to pray out loud in each other's presence. It seems hard to break through the "sound barrier." But work at it! Be patient with one another. The benefits will far outweigh any initial embarrassment or sense of strangeness. When you and your mate can freely talk to God in each other's presence, it is sure proof that God has really become a member of your family — and that is what He longs to be.

One last word on this subject. Never again rely solely on your own effort and ability to make your marriage a success. No marriage can ever be what God intends it to be apart from God's supernatural grace. The commitment you have now made to your mate and your marriage has made that grace available to you in a measure that you have never known before. Avail yourself of it freely! God has told us, "My grace is sufficient for you, for My power is perfected in weakness" (2 Corinthians 12:9). God's grace and power will see you through every difficulty that arises. If you feel perplexed, discouraged, inadequate, trust God for an extra measure of grace and power, just then and there. Expect to see Him work — in ways, perhaps, you could never have imagined. Expect to see Him change whatever needs to be changed — you, your mate, the whole situation. He will not fail you.

Commitment to God's People

The third area of relationship that we have dealt with in this book is that which we have called *koinonia* — the sharing of your life with God's people. For true spiritual fulfillment you need this kind of relationship. Without it, you can never be all that God intends you to be. This is equally true for single people and for married couples.

All of us need to be part of something larger than ourselves.

In 1 Corinthians 12:13—27 Paul compares individual believers to the various parts that make up a single body. He explains that no part can function effectively on its own. Each needs the others. "And the eye cannot say to the hand, 'I have no need of you;' or again the head to the feet, 'I have no need of you' " (verse 21). As individual believers, we can only achieve true fulfillment and wholeness by entering into a committed relationship with other believers in such a way that we can, together with them, function as a single body.

A relationship of this kind is not optional. It is essential for our own spiritual well-being. Let us look once more at a verse that has been quoted earlier: "But if we walk in the light as He Himself is in the light, we have fellowship (*koinonia*) with one another, and the blood of Jesus His Son cleanses us from all sin" (1 John 1:7).

The introductory "if" confronts us with two related facts of spiritual experience. First, the primary evidence that we are walking in the light is that we have *koinonia* with one another. If we do not have this relationship of *koinonia* with other believers, it is normally evidence that we are not walking fully in the light. Second, if we are not in the light of *koinonia,* we no longer experience the continuous cleansing of the blood of Jesus, which alone can keep us pure and free from sin.

Our responsibility for regular fellowship with a group* of committed believers is stated again in Hebrews 10:24—25:

(24) And let us consider how to stimulate one another to love and good deeds,

(25) not forsaking our own assembling together, as is the habit of some, but encouraging *one another;* and all the more, as you see the day drawing near.

Here again, we have two related truths: the first, we are responsible to stimulate and encourage one another; the second, we can do this only if we do not forsake "our own assembling." This last phrase obviously takes it for granted that all of us will be related to a group which we can properly call "our own assembly."

The essential step which brings us into this kind of relationship is the same that brings us into proper relationship with God

*I use the word "group" because it has a broad meaning. Such a group may be what would normally be called a "church." Or it may function in a different way. There is room for considerable variety.

or with our mate. It is *commitment* — not just to another individual, however, but to a group who are themselves united in mutual commitment. If you have already made the first two commitments dealt with in this chapter — to God and to your mate — you should follow that with this third form of commitment — to a group of fellow believers.

Unfortunately, it is not always easy, in contemporary Christendom, to find a group who are practicing real, mutual commitment on a sound scriptural basis. However, if you acknowledge to God your need to identify with such a group, and then go on to seek Him diligently for His direction, you can be confident that He will show you what to do. Remember that God has promised to reward those who seek Him (Hebrews 11:6). If you are sincere and earnest in seeking Him, you will receive your reward.

As a guideline to recognize the kind of group that will fulfill your need, here are nine questions you should ask before you make any definite commitment:

1. Do they honor and uplift the Lord Jesus Christ?
2. Do they respect the authority of Scripture?

3. Do they make room for the moving of the Holy Spirit?
4. Do they exhibit a warm and friendly attitude?
5. Do they seek to work out their faith in practical day-to-day living?
6. Do they build interpersonal relationships among themselves that go beyond merely attending services?
7. Do they provide pastoral care that embraces all your legitimate needs?
8. Are they open to fellowship with other Christian groups?
9. Do you feel at ease and at home among them?

If the answer to all or most of these questions is "yes," you are "getting warm." Continue to seek God, however, until you receive definite direction from Him.

Remember that you probably will not find "the perfect group." Furthermore, even if you did, you could not join it, because after you did, it would no longer be perfect!

Finally, here is a word of encouragement, but also of warning, from Psalm 68:6:

God makes a home for the lonely;
He leads out the prisoners into prosperity,
Only the rebellious dwell in a parched land.

If you are "lonely," God will place you in a spiritual "home" — a family of Christian brothers and sisters, united in mutual commitment to one another. If you are a "prisoner" — of circumstances or evil forces — God will deliver you and bring you out into freedom. But — and here is the warning — if you are "rebellious," you will continue to "dwell in a parched land."

Ultimately, the only barriers that can keep you from finding the kind of *koinonia* you need will be your own inner attitudes of pride, or selfishness, or unyielding individualism. Ask God to show you if there are any such barriers in your life; and if there are, to break them down.

In Psalm 27:4, David gives utterance to the deepest longing of his soul:
One thing I have asked from the LORD, that I shall seek;
That I may dwell in the house of the LORD all the days of my life, . . ."

Do these words of David express the deep longing of your soul? If so, why not echo them in a prayer of your own?

Once again, if you feel able to pray in your own words, do that. But if you prefer a prepared prayer, you may use the following:

Lord, I am lonely and unfulfilled, and I acknowledge it. I long to "dwell in your house," — to be part of a spiritual "family" of committed believers. If there are any barriers in me, I ask you to remove them. Guide me to a group where this longing of mine can be fulfilled, and help me to make the needed commitment to them. In the Name of Jesus.   *Amen.*

OTHER BOOKS BY DEREK PRINCE

**For a complete catalog of
books and audio and video cassettes
write:**

Derek Prince Ministries—International
P. O. Box 300
Fort Lauderdale, Florida 33302-0300
U.S.A.

B31/11-93/1M/LRP